Farewell, America the Beautiful

Stephan Brown

With deep gratefulness for all the brave souls who, for better or worse, may have loved this impossible rascal during his time within "the blink".

2023 First Printing
Farewell, America the Beautiful

Copyright © 2023 by Stephan Brown

Back cover portrait: Emile Klein

Pen and Ink Art, page 8: Shea Cadrin

ISBN: 979-8-218-96945-5

10 9 8 7 6 5 4 3 2 1

All rights reserved.

Printed in the United States of America

Contents

Proem to the Poems: A Word about "Poetry" 5
Prelude 9
Sap Rising in a Blessed Sun 11
Satyrs of Spring 13
Scent 15
words like rivers run 16
Boston, Bound—From an Island in Thailand 18
Buck buck moon, and dewey does 21
Creme de Paradis 23
Curmudgeon come rumbling 26
Daffodils !(circa 1975) 27
Delphinium Seeds 29
Echo 30
Evening window 31
Falling to pieces 32
Grief holds the heart so tightly bound 33
Hearts Beat Beating 34
Herbcrafting, Wordcrafting 36
How does a farmer say goodbye to his land ? 38
I will not read the papers today 40
In small rooms 41
In wee hours, waking 42
Lament to Goddesses Green 44
Lo, Lovely Lady 45
Lo, the nights now longer lay 46
Love's Phoenix 48
Lusty Lament of the Lady and Lord 49

March Wind on the Great Outer Beach 52
Miss Harriet Ellis 54
My sun my son 56
Old Soul Knowing 58
Poem in October 59
Poem in November 60
Running away 62
Seeds and Doves 63
Summer Lilies 65
Sunrise, Nauset Beach Bight, October 23 2016 68
The Old Backpacker 69
The poet's life 70
The words will come 72
To a soldier crying 74
To all the weary warriors 76
Truro night, 1968 79
Welcome, Miss Eyva Jayne 80
Work day done 82
Why "Farewell, America the Beautiful"? 84

Proem to the Poems: A Word about "Poetry"
... and this first collection.

I have found, in my lengthy lifetime of reading and writing poetry, many a style in the presentation of an arrangement of words for a reader to absorb and find meaning and, ideally, pleasure within.

In earlier centuries, rhymes and rhyme schemes were of capital importance. The 'Byron-Keats-and-Shelly' generation so revered this style. Along came e.e.cumings, Alan Ginsburg, Ferlinghetti and rhyme flew away. So also, for the most part, did rhythm. And so did the 'music' of thoughtfully chosen and placed words.
Poetry became solely cerebral.

Then along dusty Highway 61 from Hibbing, Minnesota came the poetic troubadour Robert Zimmerman. With 'chips' from Paul Bunyan's mighty axe dusting his shoulders like dandruff came 'chip-on-his-shoulder' Bob Dylan. And the poetry world moved again upon its great axis. For in the masterpieces of Dylan, the eternal dance of music and poetry became a memorable revolution, and they will endure as do those of Homer, Hopkins, Elliot, Thomas, and so many others. Not quite the cacophony of an orchestral 'warm up' (cumings, Ginsburg, et. al.), and not the ordered beauty of a symphonic piece (the "romantic poets"), Dylan's smashing and mashing, weaving and intuitive tickling of music and poetry spun a web around the world.

The offerings that you are about to read are diverse, oft perverse, like human beings :
Sometimes ordered and serene. Sometimes cacophonic. Sometimes rhythmic. Sometimes rhyming. Sometimes cerebral. Sometimes playful. Sometimes happy, sometimes sad. Oftentimes mad.

I had considered arranging them in a 'normal' framework of theme, or time, or place, but upon reflection, I reconsidered. For is not a poem an entity unto itself, unrelated to previous or following expressions of self and thought ? And so I have once more rebelled against order and placed these expressions within the book with no 'rhyme nor reason'— I simply let the computer arrange them alphabetically !! Ha ! Exceptions are the first four poems, which give a flavor of the meal to come. Interestingly, four of the more humorous poems begin with "L" (for "Laughter"?!?)
I leave it to you, dear reader, to make your own arrangement from, I suppose, most liked to less liked. "Up to you !", as they love to say in Thailand. And— have fun !

I have humorously called myself "the world's oldest virgin poet" as, in my now-seventy seven years of writing poetry in this Great Life, I have never sought to publish. So take my chastity now ! dear reader. I am finally ready to be shared ! If it "was as good for you as it was for me", we will be blissing ! (are you smiling ?!?)

To 'take the temperature' of you contemporary readers of poetry, I would be so appreciative if you would choose your favorite six poems herein and tell me, and the world, of your selections, as this is about poetry preference in general among we souls living precariously within this "blink in the spectrum of Time".

Any further elucidations are, of course, graciously welcomed. I do believe that collaboration, the sharing of ideas, is germane, and stimulating (!), to creativity.

With appreciation beyond reason— S.B.Brown
Terceira Island, Portuguese Azores, October 4, 2023

Prelude
to the loss of my poetic publishing virginity at age 77

Cock and Fox

One day there came upon my farm, a fox. I was not there to see this fox, but the apothecary, working my herbal pharmacy, swore that the fox was attacked by one of my cocks. I had, myself, never seen such a brazen cock attack a fox in all my years (which, verily, wax great). Thus must I rely upon another's eyes for account.

My apothecary, a fine artist as well as creative herbalist, later penned her bent of the farmyard event, which now graces the face, the contrasting cover, of this father's tale of suns and lovers.

Poetry is a tale told by an absentee witness who missed sight of 'the fox and the cock', and thus must rely upon report of Fates, who tell of the world through magnified eyes, through a ripple-tinted window of very old pane... Interesting, this life. These lives we have lived. How we give(d). What we see(d).

You are the palette. Words are the brush filled with color. The cocky fox leaves a footprint : a glint, a hint — varmint !

Sap Rising in a Blessed Sun

March moon waxes in a wide black sky
Star-filled in lovers' dreams
And plant spirits sleeping, still
Burled and buried in gritty blankets brown and black,
Roll in their roots.

The slumbering soul glides skyward
In a weave of dreams :
The secret self. And love swells
In rooty cells, stirs the earth,
Moves in a myriad of wild and wanting thoughts,
Ascends the quickening stems, attends
To April's aching air— O hear !
Hear ! As desire draws near as the knee !
The pinions shiver, shudder in a rage of procreation
O hear me ! slaves of desire,
Slaves of sweet Nature's knee-weak nectar !
And now licentious yearning, turning toward May ;
Now in waning April remembering May
Forthcoming, coming forth, coming toward May
O god! we adore this rite of Spring ! We
Ache in this passion, this
Sap rising in a blessed sun !

In our secret heart we are the flower,
We are the stamen, the pistil,
The ovary wall glistening, the

Sticky embrace of the bee,
The seed that swells,
The silky rush toward heaven ...
O April— O hear ! Oh god ! Oh
Hear as Desire draws near as the knee—
This rage! this rush! sweet nectar
Coming forth— coming toward May!

Oh how we obsess in this rite of Spring! How we
Ache in this passion, this trembling, this mad sap
rising in a blessed sun !

Satyrs of Spring

Through the magisterial ministry of March
Satyr spirits of Spring are sleeping
in crystal palaces of frost   in garden soil.

Their Winter wet dreams will stir
within this dark womb of slumbering Ceres,
subtle and silent, patient in winter waiting.

As the waxing warmth of April breathes upon the land,
small tender tendrils emerge, the waking dream flutters.

Now ! Oh, on a cello day in May ! when Apollo's golden
   sun floods the land
and the erotic aroma of newly-turned earth brings
   quivering erections
of life and joy within husbandry's heart...

Now then, in an amorous setting forth, does the farmer
   take his wife to field ,
Lays with her upon the ground, and plants his seeds...
                                                    his promises.

We are brown seeds bursting and green leaves weeping joy
As we break into a new world of eternal and infinite
   possibility—
transition to sun-soaked green, sweet kiss— metamorphosis !

Now spent, Love's Pan pipe falls from the careless hand,
and the husband slides sweetly back to the loving arms
of Spring slumber,   you…
                    and the promises that now you keep.

About Satyrs (from an unknown internet source) :
Praxiteles gives a new interpretation on the subject of free and
carefree life. Instead of an elf with pointed ears and repulsive
goat hooves, we face a child of nature, pure, but tame and
fearless with brutal instincts necessary to enable it to defend
itself against threats. Above all though, the Satyr with flute
has a small companion, which shows the deep connection with
nature, the soft whistle of the wind, the sound of gurgling
water of the crystal spring, the birds singing, or perhaps the
singing of a melody of a human soul that feeds higher feelings.
As Dionysian creatures they are lovers of wine and women, and
they are ready for every physical pleasure. They roam to the
music of pipes, and they love to chase maenads or bacchants
(with whom they are obsessed, and whom they often pursue)
or, in later art, dance with the nymphs

Scent

I carry you like a scent :
it saturates all that I do, all that I think.
It is provocative, musky— it excites me always !
It is not removed in the bathing.
Cleaning my skin only makes it stronger.
Your scent mixes with mine and becomes
even more powerful, like a potent herbal formula--
blending, the synergy lifting its healing possibilities
into a heaven, beyond the known,
              beyond the rational,
                            beyond belief.

I adore every smell of you-
your breath, your hair, your love place.
My heart pounds like that of a wild animal !
jaguar, cheetah, gazelle
in a final leap, jaws wide, blood racing,
the moment of ecstasy an instant away !!

The mind is irresponsible, derelict—
sweet Nature's slave in this eternal pattern
of male and female uniting, this joining of egg and seed,
yin and yang, penis and vagina, heaven and earth.

Only Time, in her inevitable, merciful erosion,
will abate the strength of your scents.

words like rivers run

words like rivers run
in their cascades of days
or born in the night from restless dreams, and fright.

sometimes slow through valley meadow's flow,
words rise to meanings like fat trout feeding ;
sometimes be they in free-fall toward rock,
free fall, free verse-- at constriction they baulk.

some do they sing with the stream-polished stones .
some do they murmur at midnight with moans .
some do they dance in the warm waters wild .
some do they hum in Mum's sweet lullabies .

words like rivers run
through works well-wrought in poem, and tome ;
off'ring myriad voice through mindful choice,
of many a clattering consonant
which, with shapely verb, superbly formed
with the mind's deft fingers,
fashion a thought …that lingers !

now, begin they their long meadow run
from spring spilling forth from earth;
down mountain, through forest
across valley and lea
in quest for the sea,
through sadness and mirth,

via heart, hearth, and home
wanderingly these wobbly words wend...
                              Attend !

Boston, Bound—From an Island in Thailand
(a memory of the Great Blizzard of 2015)

On an island in Thailand I sleepily sat
in my bungalow reached by a neat white-bleached beach;
As I sat sipping java (or was it pina colada?!)
I thought of those bro's I had left in the throes
of ice-caked cold blows, and mountainous snows.

Dear Boston! the town of the beans and the Bruins
Was buried alive, 'twas a city in ruins!
From the Quabbin's big lake to the tip of the Cape
Massachusetts could NOT cop a break from the flake!

So with "Dividend Miles" to the warm "Land of Smiles"
I left frozen Logan, like a Wampanoag hogan
Buried beneath winter's shivering sheath.
'Twas but hours 'fore storm, and I — heaven born!
'Bove a landscape forelorn, toward a morning more warm.

The very next night as I sweated in Bangkok
(sipping Thai beer by the pool— are you shocked?!?)
Boston was socked by another white shock!
The "Home of the Pats" was sure taking it's knocks.

It pummeled! it plundered! it ravaged and thundered!
With winds howling high in the low leaden skies.
For the way that the city was anesthetized
This "storm of the cent'ry" would be balladized
By weatherman prophets waxing theophilosophic.

On Comm Ave. and Newbury, Marlborough, Beacon—
People imprisoned, the city was freakin' !
The Southeast Expressway was hardened like clay,
as was "Emerald Necklace", and dear Rose's Greenway.

Battered and broken and so badly bound,
She narry could budge, there was narry a sound;
Not in feet, but in "Smoots" did the white fluff pile high
On the bridges of Hahvud, Mass. Ave., Tobin, Zakim
The snow Smoots was packin', and no one could track 'em.

In the decades ahead will the story be said
of the winter that kept people long in their beds?
Will we have yet another of those "boomer" generations ?
Because folks chose warm beds 'stead of cold flagellations ?

So I'll close this tome poem with a hope that you'll note
That the feared "climate change" may be not so remote;
Buenas Aires to Beijing, Warsaw to Welch Wales,
We see massive movements in mountains and vales.
The oceans' great drifts, in the airs above- shifts,
Are frostin' our Boston, e'en Atlanta, and Austin.

From Waban to Quabbin, Mattapan to Cape Ann,
Let's all join together and do what we can.
'Meffuhd', Ruveeah, Dawchestah, Glawstah—
For our boys and our girls a New World we shall fostah.
From the mess made 'fer shur' with our toys that perdure.
From Adams to Chatham, (did you hear what I said?)
Let's prepare our towns for transitions ahead !

I'll leave you with that— so long ! bye! peace ! and ciao !
I'm in for a swim at my fine Thailand island.
I'm thinkin' of y'all in the frozen Bay State
And hoping the terrible snows will abate
Before I come home in a few months time
And begin to sow seeds in more temperate clime.

Buck buck moon, and dewey does

It IS the month of the buck ! buck ! moon !
Following the green reachings of the "Strawberry Moon"
  of June
in the misty humidity of once-dry July's :

A new ecology, a new biology brewing soon in the
Buck buck boys and dewey does of summer soft evenings
With their whispered sweet solicitations—ah! celibacy's
  abdications !

But oh— how the birds are so gay, these queer days :
Filling the evening with melodious trilling of altered
  songs,
a licentious longing, a sterile dreaming of love and
  affection—
Love's resurrection .

Boys after bucks. The buck buck moon .
Girls after does, with their strawberries glistening in
  moonlight.

The slow rising of the "Buck Moon" comes soon.
The sweet juice of the strawberry fruit dewily dampens
The doe's seductive pursuit— other does.

Worlds have changed :
The musky breath of insemination belies a procreation
within the conjugal buck buck bed ,

the dewy, downey sheets of does in heat.

Ah, willing gods ! Oh, lusty goddesses quaking tonight !
Wherefore art thou in thy soul's wandering night ?
In this ethereal moment when one soul seeks birth, and
　human light ?
a world of love and joy and buck-doe boys ? Where ?

There ! There !!

Birdsong, bucksong, downbeat does… filled and trilling
　still !

There ! And there !!

Creme de Paradis

In a small village, French, par le nom Paradis
Lives a wonderful woman— Amerie;
Her skin is so lovely, men fall at her knee,
Her virtues? attend ! I will pen them !

Her secret to health is food quite quintessential,
And medicinal plants in large part;
Yes, from the dear plants, she extracts what's essential
For conquering Troy— and mens' hearts !

By night and by day, her radiance displays
A health that does come from within;
And from her dear garden there come, beg your pardon,
The herbs that do nourish and soften her skin.

Calendula dear is a plant without fear
With it's sunny sweet petals of gold;
It helps bring relief to a heart feeling grief
By helping the soul feel more wholesome and bold.

But be not remiss, there IS more than this!
Her virtues are profound and neat —
For she heals damaged skin, from without and within,
And bacteria bad will 'beat feet' !

The hip of the Rose is quite truly a fruit
Holding the seeds for it's babies;
And within those dear seeds, are the oils that do please
The dry skin of Life's older ladies.

Oil from the fruit of the Coconut tree
Is filled with constituents healing;
Their choice is to moisten and soften quite often,
And thence give your skin a fine feeling appealing.

"Yo ho" ! for Jojoba, the oil most like our mantle's,
It helps to repair wear and tear from the sun;
Replaces the texture that dryness dismantles,
Healing in godlike manner Apollonian.

Oh my! Coco butter makes young hearts to flutter,
Recalling their days at the beach;
Smearing gobs of this 'yummy' over buttocks and tummy
(Being coy to avoid places just out of reach...)

What can I say of the butter of Shea
From the island of far Madagascar ?
There is none to compare to its properties rare,
From Akar to old Zanzibar.

And fin'lly comes one from the Land of the Sun—
The islands Hawaii, with Mauii and Mahi Mahi;
Macadamian oil is a nut oil quite royal—
Its use may induce a feeling 'tres douce'.

Now, oils called 'essential' are quite preferential
For adding aroma appealing;
But beyond this great gift is their power to lift
Up the spirits from basement to ceiling !

Rose is the fragrance of love and the heart,
Helichrysum heals skin like no other;
And Sandalwood's there for the mind to share
With 'significant other', a friend, or a lover.

I hope that this balm keeps you lovely and calm,
And keeps you progressing, un-stressing;
For the plants are a blessing addressing distressing
Times that need careful and tender caressing.

So, be "in your skin", treat your skin from within,
But also use topical treasures :
To help you to be like Amerie de Paradis—
And, who knows?! have some romantic pleasures...

Be happy. Smile often !

Ingredients : farm-grown flowers of Calendula, infused into Sweet almond oil; cold-pressed oils of Rosehip seed, Hawaiian Kakui nut, Jojoba seed, Castor bean ; Coconut oil ; Coco butter ; Shea butter ; essential oils of Rose, Sandalwood, Helichrysum.

Curmudgeon come rumbling

An old curmudgeon come rumbling I,
grumpily bludgeoning bumbling thy;
Offending my foe and friend quite alike,
Sons and daughters, elders and tykes.

Can't help it, 'tis simply the nature of Man—
verbal, bi-pedal, but of Caliban clan.
'We' should say "sorry" for being so sour,
raining upon your parade— dour shower
of bellicose verbs, and words quite offensive
instead of uplifting, extensive, and pensive.

Shame on me, and my daft royal "we",
Some young small wee should on me take a pee !

Daffodils ! (circa 1975)

"Daffodils" she said
"I want to set spring bulbs in the ground ,
the ones with the paper-peeling, brown-skinned sides ,
the double ones that look like buffalo horns .
Yes , the ones with green tips
that will struggle through the gimpy frost of March
and burst upon the planet
with the Chinook winds of April.

I want to see the stems extend   and reach   and divide ;
form green-gold buds that hang in ebullient air like un-
opened umbrellas .
I want to see them open in Spring rain ,
become drunk and light-headed ,
bob and weave and laugh in sunlight .

I want to see daffodils feed on the sun ,
take sunshine into the earth to feed their young .
I want to know that in the damp womb
those bulbs will fatten and bear young ,
will gestate in cool earth beneath a summer sun ..
Yes , I want to know that I have families of daffodils
living beneath the lawn ..

I do want to know that life goes on ,
that each year we come again
in greater profusion than before   and
I want to be assured each Spring that daffodils do not die

beneath the cold and iron weight
of Winter's heart-freezing frost ... "

Delphinium Seeds

An October moon penetrates the shell of delphinium seeds
cracking in the cold air of midnight.
They will hold and remember moonlight.
They will drop to Earth and sink
beneath leaves by winter.

They sleep in December..
They forget in January..
These lovely and forgotten seeds
slumber through February..

We will think of them in our private dreams.
We will think of them as we harvest bay scallops.
We will think of them as we burn locust logs
in iron stoves.

The dream of many springs will wake them in April,
make them aware of their young bodies as
skins crack, the tender proboscis
sets forth its foot, the head lifts slowly toward morning.

We enjoy this setting forth.
We enjoy this adventure as we break soil.
We are delphinium seeds in a winter garden.
We feel words stirring within us.
We await the birth of moonlight

Echo

you are the echo
you are the voice that returns time and again
you are the sound repeating
you are the thought that reproduces
you are the dream that cannot be realized
you are the hope that rides the thrown-stone ripples
across mountain lakes where none can go

you are the echo
you are the disturbance that awakens the sleeping lion
you are the lone climber who seeks high places
beyond echo

you are the echo
the sound repeating
the dream, the stone, the ripple repeating
the flight across chasms of infinite depth
the light that leaps into heavens again
and again and again and again.....

echos and echos and echos and echos
repeating, returning, reproducing a yearning
a return to the source of the unbridled dream--
mountain lake, a glassy stillness of silence
cradled by mountains, by heavens, by the silent climber
a place before voice
a time before sound
a world before echos

Evening window
(1960's or 70's)

It is hard for he to write of peace—
the rocking chair soul, the
frail fold of knuckles old
in a wrinkled lap.

Of peace it is hard for she to write—
she that has known so little
of the gentle breeze in an evening window,
curtains making ghosts in the golden light,
the rocking chair a-twitch,
and whisps of grey hair.

Falling to pieces

On Cape Cod does a wild summer-thunder wind
break pine and locust branches
falling to pieces.

In Portugal, Spain, France small villages burn to ashes
in whirlwinds of flame dancing, singing.

In Afghanistan, Italy, Thailand floods swirl above the knees
of beasts, prophesying.

Someone is angry. Very angry.
Transgressors dumb to their rationalizations, protestations.

The piper shall be paid.
The meek re-inherit Earth—
and dearth.

How does one feel who has fallen from a plane ?
or Grand Canyon cliff (as many do),
thrashing wildly at thin air,
the terror of no-way-back
as so do we now watch helplessly
the Earth, and we
falling to pieces.... ?

Grief holds the heart so tightly bound

Grief holds the heart so tightly bound
That some, in myriad struggles and flailings dire,
breathe not the gift of a sweet and opiate air.

Heavens, please release these bark-bound limbs from bonds
of flesh and sodden earth, dust and flood, freeze and thaw.
Gift relief from grief and cords that clasp the saddened
   heart.

Why, that some few must feel the blows of Life's recurrent
   strikes ?
these bolts of pain ? and why such profusion
upon the humbled soul ? Why have some come to bear
the greater share of grief ?

I sigh brief relief in this fair and stilly air,
that grief has not yet returned my outbound prayer
of compassion to those seeking sanctity
beneath the weight of their consuming gravity.

Hearts Beat Beating

Moved heart hear my song, my sweet song
My dream song, my sweet dream song
Soft song of sweetness calling
Softly the words to mind
To mind the soft words, to mind
The call of sweet love to
Mind the joyful heart

Hearts beat beating
The quick heart beating the
Drum of the soul beat beating
Beating in slumber's pure air beating
Beating for the soul to be born beating beat
Beating in the birth of the child beating
In the childheart beating beating

For the sacred ages of Adam beating
For the endless ages of Eve
Beating in the pulse of the heavens
Heavens in the pulse of a man
Millennia of men in my pulse
My pulse the mirror of love's shining lust and

You, your face, your eyes your
Secret self, your sacred soul your eyes
In the mirror seen as though
No heart had beat
Before this moment.

In this moment—
This blissful, blinding moment of
Holding your face of
Finding behind your eyes
Love's needs, love's lusts, lost loves
And the wild and wanting ways of
Life's insatiable longing for love—
The revelation and perfect penetration
Of your most secret harmony....
Need love, lust love, lose love.... Lost loves

Herbcrafting, Wordcrafting
Hours Mis-spent in Gastronomic Thought

I have mis-spent many an idle hour trying to turn a word
on a sizzling spit of winsome wit.

In that I prefer wild game and weeds,
my words were far less apt to please
the tongue of those who staidly sipped
more common fare brought soft to lip.

Turning to a perfect doneness, possibly pleasing ,
or, at the least, another's palate appeasing ;
was never reason to use a soft seasoning —
for the tepid tastes of domesticated places,
was not in my favor, as one born to wild flavor.

The words that I turned were not fain from the farm,
but more from the forest, river, stream, and the sea :
more from wild 'virons, ruled by Diana's and Chiron's,
where savor and flavor run pure, clean and free.

In the rising aromas that boast verbal diplomas,
would I seek to raise pilgrim and lit'rary taste
to ethereal heaven that received them in grace ;
from strong, sucking roots, and tender green shoots,
winding wraiths, turning words, in realms of bright green ,
would i braise herbal potage not yet tasted or seen :
they were strong on the tongue, and it's neighbor, the mind—
associations aligned in refined humankind !

Our great ancient seeds become nourishing weeds :
Yea, myriad seeds soon become healing leaves
Which turn vibrant colors, blazing orange and red,
before falling to ground, and a rich compost bed.

So same with our words, spread with love in good soil,
will become, from the strum of the heavens, unmoiled.
They will please the mind's palate like leek, beet, or squash;
and heal like calendula, mint, or cohosh.

Once was I, then, a wildcrafter of words,
a rake shaking tinctures in diurnal rite,
extracting the essence, the plants' great percipience
that satisfies hunger and heals what lacks balance.

Many balms would i blend for the body and spirit,
some done with herbs, and some sung with words :
with wild-gathered herbs , and musical words
I could often allay a distressed mind's sad dismay.

Perhaps one day another will feed upon herbs,
and savor these turning words... ?

How does a farmer say goodbye to his land ?
(Reflection upon a 'forced neglect' and consequent ruination ordered by a Town's Conservation Commission)

We know the words of goodbye to a wife, a husband, a
   partner, a lover,
a dog, a cat, a bird, another…
but what are the words that we can say to a farm ? a land ?
the source of our nourishment and life ? our calloused
   hand ?

I don't know. I do not know the words.
A life-long poet and wordsmith and I cannot find words,
   words !
words to say to the land that I have shepherded for fifty
   years
of my time on this earth.
There is a chasm. There is an emptiness within the cage of
   the ribs,
a darkness in a once-lit room of friends and fire and cheer.

It is a slow 'fare well, dear earth', a slow death-by-
   starvation,
a strangulation ;
For the land had become a part of the blood, the lymph,
   the spleen ;
it made the heart to beat, and raise the old bones to the
   breakfast table.

What does a farmer do when his farm is taken away ?

What does he do ? What can he say ? Pray ?
Is it prayer that brings redemption ? answers the questions ?
Makes sense of the non-sensible ? absolves the tresspass of power ?

I don't know. I do not know the words.
I cannot pronounce the sylables.
I have no verbs, no adjectives, no help from what I thought myself so adroit, so nimble, so cunning at juggling in pure air, and
letting them fall gracefully upon a page with feeling and sense.
All gone. All empty. All a void.

My throat is dry. I have a headache. May I please be excused ?

Who will care for my land now ? care for my vulnerable child ? my friend ? my tempestuous partner ? my hovel ? my hermit life ?
I am no longer connected. I drift aloft. And alone.

How do I say "goodbye" to this land ? this beautiful and fruitful land that provided for so many ? gave freely of her bounty ? her protection ?
This perfection now is riddled with a human infection— pride : Humanity's calamitous imperfection.

I will not read the papers today

Warm a-bed with the gas fire on and a first
snow outside my "Currier and Ives" windows :
the gardens and snow-felted Pitch pines,
Cryptomeria, Maple, Ginkgo, Oak.

I shall not read the papers today, as I have done
for decades and myriad dawns.
I do not want to hear of the shootings and accidents
and corruption, and the greed of humans
on this pure and white break-of-day dawn.

No…. this snow-silent, shadow-dappled dawn I will learn
   how to take a boat trip from Yunnan in China to Luang
   Prabang in Laos.
I will find a guesthouse in Siem Riep near Ankor Wat.
I will transport my self and my imaginary partner to
   the gardens of Kyoto, and sip tea watching the delicate
   branches of Japanese maples and Katsura drop dew.

I will not read the papers today…

In small rooms

On such thick nights moisture penetrates the skin,
sinks beneath the newly-turned earth,
is absorbed by the epidermis of seeds
causing soft, subterranean explosions..

The moon hides ! Is afraid to produce moonbeams !
On such nights the bark of the brain thickens—
becomes cork-like, crustacean,
protective of the inner rooms..

In the dark corridors of deep forests
the ghosts of rabbits and moles
weave among dying plants, become
almost living..

In small rooms people look about, try to think ;
they close one eye and hum songs learned in infancy..
Many tunes come back to us as we die
in small rooms.

In wee hours, waking

In wee hours, waking, approaching dawn ;
in wee foggy hours when thoughts are drawn
sadly 'round the trembling heart—
a wee vine seeking a strong support.

This be the time of contemplation,
loneliness, and deep rapport ;
a soothing void, an inclination
drifting toward a farther shore.

A Junebug bats the summer screen,
and we, comatose, 'tween sleep and dream.

Stillness.
Withered needles of fir fall free
through silent forest air. Be.

This, the twining time when one can climb
and feel within the whining bones,
the blain, the pain, of time alone :
ephemeral hour at the edge of night
when the wee hours wane
and the day doth gain,
in bright Aurora's birth of light.

Oh human plight ! That we in natural right
so briefly pass, our bones indict.
Why that we, so cursed with contemplation,

be strapped by bounds of Life's demarcation ?

And how shall go we ? in peace ? gracefully ?
beneath the sea of briney time ?
How broach the Sea of Forever and sink,
with acceptance and joy, in but a blink,
'neath the waters of Lethe to release.... relief ?

Lament to Goddesses Green
(the poor male's plight)

Oh you ! You herbal wenches writhing green !

Calamity of the Cosmos, and

Brightest sparks littering the dark Heavens
with the sparkling, trailing tails of meteors !

Lo, what blinding light through yonder Artemisian fields
doth set the deep nights ablaze with cascading Calendula
suns?!

At this very moment, in your leaf-green stirrings,
ye do stoke the fragile hearts of men !
blaze through the veins of many a worthy,
and helpless, suitor !

Strong men may lay before you on the painful spikes of
humiliation.

Suffering men feign food, sweet repose,
and all comforts of life
to be your devoted pilgrim, your supplicant -

and father of your children.

Lo, Lovely Lady

Lo! Lovely lady do lade thy liege
with Love's lonely ligature— trust.
'Tween lily-like limbs,
O Lust— lay thy siege !
Yea, entwine thine lion in lines of lust;
From luscious lacuna dispense Love's sweet scents,
From labial lips—Love's lubricous lure!

The man, the mane, rock-hard— love's bane !
Love's willing lunge! (and lust's only cure!).
Ah, luxuriant lolling in the lion's liar
'neath labyrinthian linens, languishing long.
In lambent breath from warm, soughing breasts—
the heart sings soft it's silvery songs
Of love-tainted lust, and sad loss of trust.

Lo, the nights now longer lay

Days darken sooner now, here on the great Cape
of Thoreau's winsome wandering
down the pouty outer shore
toward it's curled terminal fist of piney land
and wind-whipped Bay State sand.

In these late-autumn hours when
the poultry have ceased their molt,
and parsnips be set to pull
from the arms of the cooling earth;
one worms a winding way to the heartwood of the soul,
there to prepare a long winter's night of still introspection.

Here we list with the roll and ride of the rising tide,
   storm-swelled
and frothily licking its high-water bound of beach.

How ambitious are we old ones ! here on a darkening shore,
late October and summer's serendipity but a memory,
thinking we could possibly light the wild night sky with
bright dreams of a sun-drenched Australian wench
bearing brimming bottles of foaming beer
buoyed before a buxom breast spilling forth it's luscious
   beckoning call.
Oh sweet foolish male-ache of eternal and unrequited desire !

Yet, with years marching ever on, and that dear, stirring sun
settling slowly in the once-loquacious loins

of a gamboling young buck always ready for rut—
We, we gentle men of greater years, of the wisdom years,
of the years of giving back... We
repose here on the pouty outer shore of the great cape
and dream... and dream... of pouty winsome wenches
bearing gifts of May flowers, spring showers.... dream...
of serendipitous summer days and summer haze ..
"There ! there ! two points off the starboard bow ! "

Days darken earlier now in the great Bay State,
beside the pouty outer shore of pilgrim pines,
the roll and ride of receding tide, serendipitous suns
burning and beckoning we the wise ones, we the gentle men,
we who dream beside storm-swelled seas,
We who retire into wild night skies,

and fall toward sleep in beds of May flowers,
spring showers, and serendipitous suns burning
in a blue June heaven ....

Love's Phoenix

Where goes the love between woman and man
When drift they apart, and hand leaves hand?
"Does it go to heaven?", as small children say?
When speaking of souls that have passed away?

"God only knows", is the gentle reply
To those who would query the reasons and why's
Of love's long endurance, or sad disappearance—
It's joys and beliefs, it's ploys and it's griefs.

Does love ever die? does it fade in the wind?
Or does it circle our souls again and again?
Where does it go if it isn't in hand?
Does it shrivel and die ? or does it expand ?!

Do we ever stop loving the one we had chosen
When warm words were shared, but now lie frozen?
Is it foolish to hope that it's never too late?
Can Heaven be found in a turning of fate?

Can love be reborn, after time has sped by,
Like the mighty Phoenix rising into the sky?
Whoever can know what the Fates hold in store
For thyself and the partner that you so adored?

Will forever you hold their dear heart to your own?
And again crave those words- "Please........ come home."?

Can love be reborn, after time has sped by,
Like the mighty Phoenix rising into the sky.......

Lusty Lament of the Lady and Lord

She nay could say "no" to the knave she knew,
But she knew he'd know if she kneeled in the nave—
That she was a nun, and of that he'd have none!
So naught did she let this knave come nigh.

His lies lay low, but they pleased like the lyre;
She lief did list' on the lies he lade.
He then levied his fee—she was laid on the lea!
Then he lanched his launch, and left by the sea...

His mettle was mean, his mein like metal;
This man of the manor displayed no manners!
For a mattoid man's mead is malmsey and mead,
Yea a Miss, a maiden, a maid to be made!

One day the dame, a lovely Dane
Began designs upon the dey
Whose demesne this doe did deign desire;
And discretely the demirep did devise
Her domination of the dey's domain.

He the erotic exosculator, she the Ephesian 'elle'—
met one day in the month of May.. (oh god, how
   romantic...).
His hale gait was great as he neared the gate
Of the wholly unholy harlot.
In a manner most male he made the moat
Of the mammonist Magdalene.

He said "I've come to woo you"
(it was actually QUITE the reverse!);
"My love for you will last weeks through"
(like snow on the desert sands!)

Our pearl seemed so pleased with the personal purl
Of the plaintiff's plaintive pleas;
Naught did he know it was naught but a show—
For she lusted his land and their leas.

The sick, wicked wretch then wrested the ranch
In a way that was wry and rank :
He gave her the ring, her checkbook did sing,
and she skipped all the way to the bank !

The subsequent scene just had to be seen,
'twas a session in sanity cession—
She filed for divorce (with a smile, of course!)
This sarcophag, schmendrick spadassin !

The divorce, of course, was a feint, a farce-
A faulty and foetid forray;
The phrase "It pays" for females in frays
of this nature was proven that day.

With a moral I'll end this pointed poem,
It's a lesson Love's lackeys should learn—

Lust is a bust, it's "love's labor lost",
and money makes maids maenad madams :
Hit the hay with your honey—Brad, Buffy, or Bunny—
You're safe if it isn't "for love nor money" !

March Wind on the Great Outer Beach

Once again am I "Baron of the Beach" ! Alone and
Lord of the tan sand sweep, creeping and accreting
Southward toward Chatham, and the Monomoy refuge.

Tonight's waves break into the teeth of an off-shore wind which
gathers it's power transiting the open sweep of Pleasant Bay.
This raging gale rams the long outer beach bight,
leaps the many legions of streaming beach grass blades
rooted upon the back shore dune ;
and teasels the blustery breakers rushing from Spain
into a hiss of salt-sea mist.
This— the outer Cape in high weather !

The marsh hawk dances, in jitterbug flight,
over the sandy back shore swales ;
dips into beach plum and rose hip hollows.
Ahh... Cape Cod in high weather !

I adore this wild sea's 'speaking-in-tongues' !
I adore the thousand languages it has heard
from those coming to its shores in myriad countries
for counsel, in sadness,
in joy, with thanks, with offerings,
                                      and in desperation.

These many-colored people, these fishermen, these city souls,
lovers bereft, grief-torn women in shawls of black
call to their friend and salty confidant —

"in sickness and in health, for richer, for poorer
til death do us part"....
                        the eternal and great Cape sea.

Miss Harriet Ellis

The year, be it 1857. My name is Jared Winslow. I am a fisherman and gatherer. I live in Provincetown, at the end of the world.
I am walking into pine dunes to find mushrooms for family, neighbors, and the Brewster Fair.
I am alone. I live alone in a small shack behind the inshore dunes along the outer reach. Some call it Helltown.
Life passes slowly. I long for love and children. There is no-one in Provincetown that I could love. I will take the packet boat down Cape on Saturday and sell at the Brewster Market Day. And perhaps I shall see Miss Harriet Ellis once again.
There are farms in Brewster, and fine crops.

Away from the noise of this town it is quiet. Still. No horses, trains, criers, blacksmith clangs, or the peal of bells at the railway station. I am learning to read words. There are some books in town.
I will learn how to write a letter to Harriet, a nice letter.
And I will even sign my name for her.

It is Saturday already ! I have stowed salted cod, shellfish, mushrooms and Autumn pies.
I cast off for Brewster, a woman in my head, a joy in my heart.
Bedroll stowed, I set sail to an aft autumn breeze that will carry me across the bay.

Tomorrow is the Brewster Market Day. I will sell my
  Provincetown harvests, or barter for Brewster carrots,
  apples, pumpkins, squashes and turnips.
And in the evening I will dance and drink cider with
  Harriet Ellis at the fair.

Harriet. Harriet whose ribbon I keep beneath my pillow.
  In a while or two I will take it out to flutter in the
  seawind coming over the northern dune to my shack in
  the soughing pines.
Harriet Ellis ! I am sailing to you this golden September
  morning
In a stiff breeze...... Brewster bound.

My sun my son
(for my son, in a cold Winter's night, 1982)

O you my sun, my son, my saviour
Sun of life, and light, and love
And you
Break in my heart gently
Like dawning sun over the
Cold teeth of Himalayas
Sun of dawn and sun of day and
Sun setting dearly
Sun of night hiding
And here, now
An angel
A fat angel with
Hair streaming, singing
A fat angel falling
Surrounded by night
This night, this precious night
In this night we wait
For love to come breaking
This night
In this long night we wait...

We have fattened our angel for
Our angel must survive the wasting wait
Through winter nights fasting

We have made our angel fat so that

She may last through this time of dearth, this
lack of life and light
And togetherness ...

Through long winter nights one feeds
on hope, one hopes
And sings, and
Says sweet songs
To night surrounding angels
Singing! we are singing in our night
We are singing for hope, and waiting for joy
And falling through night, and waiting for light
And hoping for the heart not to wither and waste
In surrounding night
In the free-fall toward love
In the fasting fall to the edge of dawn
When we see
Breaking... in the heart—
The light, the life

(Notes : This was/is for the divorced fathers, the "weekend dads", who wait all week (winter nights of the soul), sometimes many weeks, before they see their children once again, and the sun/son comes breaking. I recall so clearly my young son sleeping peacefully beside me on the cold winter's night in 1982 that this poem was born, and my dread of our parting with the rising of the sun. "Keep the faith", all you "pappa's" and "daddy's"— there ARE angels.

Old Soul Knowing

O this girl ! This tendril wraith green
Growing green 'round an old soul knowing;
An old soul seer with tender regard
For creatures, birds, and birdsong breaking
From the vanguard moments of a million years
Of love and dying, and dying of love.
This young girl green by an old soul held
in a blessed green sheath;
Wise for her years, and sad
At the way we have turned the earth
From garden to grave.
This tender girl green
This tendril wraith growing
O this girl ! this tendril wraith green growing—
An old soul seer round an old soul knowing
Her old soul held in a blessed green sheath;
In a blessed green sheath her dear soul held.

Poem in October
October 28, 2007 (revised 4/8/2011)

sitting by a fire, it's a windy hallows eve, October "hunter's
 moon" rising high through locust trees dropping leaves
in the brisky weave of a Cape bay breeze ;

the bright days wane, Autumn nights wax on,
Selene still in love with her Endymion .

I sit with smoke and fire as Wampanoag People
sat thru autumn nights long before we whites
came with pox, oxen and sheep....
and our cultural contagion.

In Autumn dreams we return to small fires kindled
in weetu's and wigwams...
        within native hearts.

Poem in November

through many centuries of sand spit seasons
did the Wampanoag People learn the scratchy speeches
and clackitty chatterings of winter winds
in the wood-frozen fingers of Cape Cod trees.

They learned the sighing, soughing songs in whispered
   piney poems
that felt like a feather in a rain-wet summer night—
" hhhwwwwoooooooohhhaaahhhshhhhh..... "

Today— a wetland wood cabin the size of a crab's hermit shell,
walls thin as clapboard, windows open all, and a rusted
   screen between this safe harbor and the blueberry bush
   world closing in.

It is miraculous! this autumn Scorpio singing, this
sexy, lubricous Leo rising in pithy pinus soughing,
'Pinus rigida' raggedly running the piney spine, the sandy
   spit, splitting the salty waters of Nantucket Sound and
   Cape Cod Bay—

Well into November, warm and sound beneath goose down
   duvet, a new Cape native listens to the treetop choir;
   awaits the shy, measured steps of the 'white tails'; the
   mumbled shuffling of the humble skunk; the siren howls
   of the coyote pack that lives here on this land
by the old tool shack out back.

Like a burning man plunging into watery salvation, I
return to my chrysalis cabin in the density of blueberry
   and bramble;
gratefully escape the madness of "proud"-spouting people,
and regress into the eons, the peace, the silence, the purity
of Time before greed.

Running away

I'm going away now, going away
to a place very, very far away :
a tundra-trek across time to an earlier day
ebullient in its youthful, pre-pubescent awakening
of tongues, that later would writhe like serpents
in their failure to speak coherently, one to another.

I am going now— this instant !
You will NOT detain me with
your seventeen reasons to wait.

I shall open my silver-shining wings to the lifting airs
of righteous flight— I am gone ! I sing !   I fly !
born upon the lifting hopes of men and women
long beaten with the whips of greed.

I will take draught now of a flower mead,
pick blackberries, newly ripened in the sun,
that grow in the back land by the pond.

In the corner of an eye the song sparrow sings;
the goldfinch clings to an amaranth stalk,
or nettle, or a thistle, in its busy day of feeding.

Anchor yourself firmly to earth and attend !
There is a choir of possibilities in the garden.
There is entertainment in every breath, every turn of the eye.
I will watch you from my lofty realm of air.
Vireos, tanagers— there ! and there !

Seeds and Doves

"I love you's" never came easily for me.
They would stick in my throat.
They'd ask to "please be excused"
and not have to come out- quite yet.
They always had a headache...
Until there was you.

With you, "I love you's" would fall from my lips
The way a dusting of new-fallen snow
Tumbles from the branches of Christmas balsams.

They would leap from my heart and dance 'round the moon !
They would cascade through the bedroom air
Like a waterfall of bright yellow begonias !

With you, my flock of "I love you's"
Would fly in happy circles through the rooms of my heart.
They'd race to see who could fly from my mouth the fastest !
And be the first to land upon your shoulder.

What a time I'd have trying to hold them all in !
I did not want them to frighten you
With their clamor, their mad beating of wings !

I wanted them to fly to you gently
With their felicitous whisperings.
They did not seem to mind me ! For too often
They'd leave my heart in anxious frenzy.

They'd fly about your ears like noisy crows.
I could not control them. There were so many !

They would fill and crowd and hurt my heart.
It was so full. I had to let some go.
I am sorry if they upset you.

I wanted so much to welcome just one of your precious doves.
I would wait by the window with seeds in my hands.
For years I waited.
For so many years have I waited
for your doves to arrive.

Summer Lilies

I'm tired of waiting. I'm tired
of waiting for the chosen one
to walk in
walk in on flames !   on burning coals !   firewalker !
courageous Lady great of spirit
I sleep with you at night
holding your cold shadow against my chest
turn.... and your arms wrap 'round me
your breasts pressing upon my back
                      rattling
my spine with crystalline tremors

At daybreak you rise in your transparency, naked
and circle the lightening room
my eyes follow longing
for you I
prepare a breakfast, fresh-baked bread
to warm your night-cold fingers
olive oil and herbs
coffee beans brought from my winter in Argentina
you watch me stir the coffee until it is, too, cold.

How we men reach out for you ! our chosen ones
perfect mates— firewalkers !

you who fill our lives with what is flesh
valuable and eternal

we bake you bread, we pour you coffee
we anoint your oil with herbs
and we watch you   aghast
evaporate with the dew
               as the morning sun
                      lifts you away
into the song of birds.

Now, let the dew and the darkness bring you
back to life !
the black hole you have left in the chest sucks
strength from the veins
we try to fill this hungry chasm
with marigolds, phlox, and big yellow begonias !
and still
          they are all sucked away

I breathe the sweet breath of the regal summer lily
and you are here again
the kneading flesh
the soft earth
the sunshine !   the light !
the twelve reasons to continue
                     the touch beneath the sheets
joy in the morning shower
         mating eyes across the table
union of fingers in garden soil
wild seeds with fire planted deeply

The black hole sucks us in and we come again
in the sweet sticky pistil
           of the summer lily

Sunrise, Nauset Beach Bight, October 23 2016

Offshore wind sprays the teasing tops of shorebound waves toward heaven this glorious Sunday dancing dawn on the long outer Cape beach bight a rising and diving of seabirds preying upon breakfast of mini fish feeding in a voracious blanket-bombing that sends frenzied spouts of seawater white into the stiff swift air this glorious Sunday dawn teasing tops and rising wraiths and torpedoing terns and gulls in their greedy feed upon the little fish in their watery grave

and on the shore

the land the cities of men and women the greedy feed goes on the large and air-born lair-born rich preying upon the small who swim in mindless swarming schools senseless of the droning terror that dives from the skies from towers of wealth and power praying not to be prey this glorious day......

The Old Backpacker

I know now that I will not be hiking the high-Andes, above
   blue lakes.
N'or even the low Rockies through mule deer brakes:
I am just an 'Appalachian man' now, plying The Trail,
   footfall measured :
Older in years. Rounded and softened by northern weathers.
Stopping more often to watch
the clouds drift over ridges, false peaks... pick up a feather....

Though there are 'a few good years' left in these creaky knees,
and the boots still have tread,
"All-day Treks'" is the name of a movie I watch in my head,
 a dream I am having,
winding through piney Georgia woods,
the Blue Ridge range under afternoon rainbow,
Susquehanna thickets, Berkshire meadows.

" I'll brew up some coffee on that overlook just off the trail.
Have a cookie, or some nuts and chocolate .
Watch Franconia Notch. Rest a tad before pushing on...

T'was that autumn hike of '59 when I first twisted the ankle.
Haunts me now and again. Slows me down for a bit.
But... we'll rally.
               Always have " . . .

The poet's life

What are the lives of poets like?
They use the word "like" often, right?
But has anyone looked to the bottom of the wordsmith's well?
Well?!? Do tell... We wait with elated breath what thou sayeth!

Are these poets contented wives and husbands?
Or are they lovers aloof ? In need of proof
that love can be a sum? a giving up of self
to another sun? a son? an "other skin" of the drum?
I am dumb to plumb this wistful wonder.

Is the security of a purity in lasting love
the bane of a bounding main that
stirs words within a poet's brain?
the true test of poet, and bard,
trying hard to excrete words onto paper
via quill and a will to expound sounds
that best express a deep loneliness of connection
with that so loved ?

I think that poets know not ! for words leap as they will
in trying trysts and dancing rills of unreason and rhyme
from these who would decline the sublime incline
of a love that flows long and deep.

Oh Dear Muse ! of patterings and pointed pens
wet with expressive ink, floundering in bogs and fens—
can you mend the woven cloth of relationship

so torn with fear of wholeness ? Of coupling ? Of release ?
Oh please ! Can you please ?

The sun has left for the day. I am alone on a vast beach
that disappears into a sea fog, eons long.
Where shall I live this salty night by the Cape's breakers ?
Shall I go south to the Chesapeake with the bluefish and bass ?
Or north with cod to Nova Scotia and the whispering winds
  of Autumn ?
Shall I tune my flute to the sea wind wild ?
And dance across chilly waters to the many lands of dreams ?
Brittany and Provence? Lao-lovely Mekong nights with warm
winds breathing downstream toward southern seas...and thee ?

A poet's life is a self-inflicted aloneness full of dreams, it seems.
Married to an endless road, an asphalt (or gravel !)
infinity;
joined in love to the fantastic sands of myriad beaches,
endless estuaries joining different worlds of being;
seeing others' worlds through the lies of a wordsmith's eyes.

I leave my beach of dreams for the day
and return to work with plants, my dear plants :
moulding them to medicine and marrying them
to those who call for help.

Oh that some tumbling pollen would find me fecund,
and dance a new life across my stage of dreams...
find me worthy of birth in a new field, flowering.

The words will come
(for Sonny, 1999)

The words will come
when you have gone to Colorado.
The words will come when I have lost your willing ear.
The words will come when you are on the road to Santa Fe,
and they will come as you approach a toll booth
and fumble for coins
the way I fumble for words
the words that should have flown to you
long before your counting and tossing of coins
and driving into the dry, Southwest morning air.

The words will come tomorrow—
after I've had time to think.
The words will come on Sunday
as I sit and read the paper, and
notice that the chair beside me is empty and does not creak.
The words will come when I
absent-mindedly go to pour you coffee
and suddenly stop...

Oh yes, I am sure they will come—
right after I place your lost earing in an envelope
that will wait patiently for your address to arrive.
I am certain they will come, like everything else in my life,
at exactly the wrong time.

They will come as I step from the shower-- squeaky clean—

refreshed, ready to start a new day.. and seeing
that your Calendula-flowered towel is not hanging
beside the wash basin.

They will come as I sit for cereal
temporarily unaware that music is not playing ;
that the house is quiet, curtains still closed,
and empty.

The words I know will come when they cannot reach you,
when you wander amazedly into the quiet red wonder of
   Bryce Canyon,
when you cannot hear them,
when you are safe
from my silent tongue
and do not come.

To a soldier crying

Sometimes a man is so sad he could cry !

"Cry ?" say women. "Crying is easy. Piece o' cake.
Crying is a walk in the park, down to the market.
Crying is baking muffins, taking a pee, combing your hair,
painting your nails"

You are women. We are men. It is not easy
for we stiff and muscular creatures,
bound by reason, chained by rational explanation,
to find that latch of release, portal to freedom,
which you find with such ease.

You wouldn't understand..... You are women.

What makes me want to cry, in my waxing years, is not
the unrequited love of woman. No --

It is hate. It is anger, intolerance, self-righteous religion,
murder in the name of some Almighty deity, some "god", some
imagined "entity", some political boundary that is revered
more than the family that lives next to me in the suburbs,
the ghetto, the wilderness, the gated liar of billionaires.

I have helped people to murder their neighbors.
I have seen governments warp balanced thought;
I have seen schools and children and women exploded into
tiny pieces of flesh and blood. Shreds of a wedding dress—
soaked in crimson dye, hanging from the branch of a tree

in the "fertile crescent",
the progenitor of "civilization"—
These. These haunt my days and my nights.

And for this, for this
                my 'grown man'
                              wants to cry.

To all the weary warriors

To all the weary warriors who have fought
to change the world — take rest.

For all of you who have sought change, dialogue,
compromise, and stayed the path of compassion—
rest your kind and weary souls

Ye who shed tears at the greed of the world—
the selfish actions that place one above another,
one people above another, one country above another—
take rest in the safe company of other compassionate
brothers and sisters of change.

Many were bombed in Beirut, but few heard or cared.
Many were killed in Paris, and the world heard !
Europeans and Americans called for bloody revenge !
When white Europeans die, the cry goes up
for revenge, carpet bombings of innocents, "military
action"—
because those innocent targets are NOT white Europeans.
They are lesser humans.

This is the Manifest Destiny of the New Millennia !
Wealthy whites shall rule all.
Wealthy whites shall dictate culture.
Wealthy whites shall judge what is "civilized", acceptable,
permitted, good, evil, and "in the best interests of the
country".

Wealthy whites shall be "PROUD" !!
Wealthy whites shall display that quality
that religions of the world detest— "Pride".
Wealthy whites shall spit "pride" and patriotism
until the civilized world of 'working poor'
shall detest them.

Can people be not "proud" ?
Say not that "I am better than you" ?
Separate one from another, father from mother.
"Co-operation not separation", heart of a nation.
Pride, power, fear— is this not clear ?
The new Manifest Destiny of the New Millennia ?

You weary warriors know
that a country needing "pride" is dying.
has lost it's way, is crying
has lost it's humanity,
sacrificed family, living in agony.

You weary warriors of change know it is so.
You heard the knell, sacrificed well, walked through Hell.
But now— as in all of sweet Nature—
you must rest, recapture the rapture, be blessed.

Regain your strength, dear sisters, dear brothers.
Take rest, nourishment, break ranks, accept thanks,

Shall we teach our children revenge ? how to hurt others ?

Shall we teach our children how to take more than another ?
Shall we teach "an eye for an eye", as part of living ?
Or "turn the other cheek", and that receiving is trumped by
　giving ?

These are the questions asked 'round the world :
The haunting "why's".
These are the questions upon which the Grim Reaper sharpens his scythe.

Truro night, 1968

In a belly of air and true breath
I caught this night early
a stir of young days
when the wild wind high as a horse's mane
brushed the summer stars
and dappled hides in the graceful heavens
raced down the dark
when shines of the prickling lights
their tiny cymbals made to the listening ear
and stars tumbled with tails
falling like notes on a scale of years

Welcome, Miss Eyva Jayne
November 4, 2013, upon the birth of my only grandchild

We welcome Eyva Jayne

Today Cronos and Gaia welcomed to their World
a small thing of beauty.
They paused in their work of Earth-building,
and beheld
in a speck of the Universe
                      a human perfection.

Miss Eyva Jayne was born this day !
Born this autumnal early morn not long beyond
a November mid o' th' night

Diurnal creatures awoke in their beds of leaf and earth
  and snow
to notice—and reverently note— the first cries of the infant
  Eyva.
Nocturnal sisters and brothers crouched in field, on forest
  floor,
on mountain shale and granite great,
in swamp, desert, cavern of ice;
and were motionless
as baby Eyva Jayne drew in her first prana breaths.

We, her family-on-Earth, welcome Baby Eyva Jayne to our
  home.
We will feed, nurture, protect this tiny tendril as she moves

toward the sun...

For you, Eyva Jayne, are the bridge, the Messenger,
the wing-footed Hermes sent
to reveal to we Earthbound, now-mortal souls
the path, the way, the Place of Pure Joy from whence you
   came.

We join with your mythical mother Maia, and father Great
   Zeus
in thankfulness for this deepest of joys that man or god
can know— the birth of a new generation of Love and Hope.

Work day done
(for our dear Great Cape Tiny Village community)

This work day now done.
I will hide away in my cave of flowers
with cool ale made blessedly-bitter
by my climbing vines of rambunctious hops.

I have had surfeit of the 'summer folk' :
the caterpillar traffic inching past my shop
en route to beach and barbecue and summer "blues"
and bass, and gentle waves, bay-breaking.

The carousel has halted for me at the peaceful hour,
and I commune with eighteen chickens, hens-but-three,
in a further recess of this abundant farm of
wild medicines, vineyard, blueberry, hop, and myriad fruit.

Here on these fertile Cape acres do I plant and promote
wild weed medicines for the common folk :
we the laboring many, we the few who look to the fields
and forests for our sustenance and for our daily meals,
daily weeds, untreated milk — our daily rejection
of mutilated foods, and unwanted injections
of which our government heartily approves.

I am comforted by the sweet scent of the summer lily
That sips from a small vase, bedside. Now five years
since I planted, with my then-wife "Wen", the bulbs that
  were to

grace us with their ebullience 'til death do us part'.
Alas— Life, and the lily, do not take to infertile soils.

Life is a trek across Tibetan mountains to escape the Chinese Terror.
Life is a free-fall toward love-- a tumbleweed bounce across an inhospitable prairie. Overcoming stasis. Finding oasis.

The work day is done

and I am one.

Why "Farewell, America the Beautiful"?

Because I am the first of my family in 393 years to leave America.

Abraham Browne arrived in 1630 on the Winthrop Fleet and settled, and helped to govern, both Watertown and Stockbridge, Massachusetts. My family fought in the Revolutionary and Civil Wars but, mercifully, did not have to participate in the many 'mass killings' to follow.

The last fifty years of my brief time upon this Earth have been spent attempting to 'create community' on Cape Cod, and leave as a legacy a lovely "Arboretum and Medicinal Plant Gardens" honoring the Universe's gift to Humanity of nourishment, health, and healing.

I have circled the globe five times through many, many countries, penetrated South America, and criss-crossed North America often over the past sixty-odd years. Among those myriad countries the beauty and diversity of the United States of America is truly spectacular. But an earlier American culture of old-fashioned "neighborliness" and co-operation is now collapsing as does any environment, or ecosystem, that is exploited by the few at the cost of the many : the human flaw that separates us from the other animals, and may be our eventual doom—Greed, and Revenge. Two qualities unique to the human species.

Thus was my original thought for the title to be —
"Farewell, America the Beautiful.
Good Bye USA Corp. "

I am saying "farewell" to America and moving to an island in the middle of "The Mighty Atlantic", and to my small sustainable community in far Northern Thailand.
I dream for my last few years...

"to dance beneath the diamond sky with one hand waving free, silhouetted by the sea, circled by the circus sands, with all memory and fate, driven deep beneath the waves.
Let me forget about today until tomorrow" *....

Blessed be. Aho.

* written, of course, by Bob Dylan

Thanks for listening —
Stephan

www.ingramcontent.com/pod-product-compliance
Lightning Source LLC
LaVergne TN
LVHW051849080426
835512LV00018B/3155